THE WORLD'S FIRST CLONED CARTOON CHARACTER

Typeset by Jonathan Downes, Peter McAdam
Cover and Layout by SPiderKaT for CFZ Communications
Using Microsoft Word 2000, Microsoft Publisher 2000, Adobe Photoshop CS.

First published in Great Britain by Gonzo Multimedia

c/o Brooks City,
6th Floor New Baltic House
65 Fenchurch Street,
London EC3M 4BE
Fax: +44 (0)191 5121104
Tel: +44 (0) 191 5849144
International Numbers:
Germany: Freephone 08000 825 699
USA: Freephone 18666 747 289

© Gonzo Multimedia MMXII

All rights reserved. Without limiting the rights under copyright reserved above, no part of this publication may be reproduced, stored in or introduced into a retrieval system, or transmitted, in any form of by any means (electronic, mechanical, photocopying, recording or otherwise), without the prior written permission of both the copyright owners and the publishers of this book.

ISBN: 978-1-908728-31-9

Roll of Honour

HENRYITES WHO HAVE CONTRIBUTED TO THE CAUSE

Tom Bennett

Jez Caudle

Nick Holmes

Keith Jeffrey

Ian Horn

Michelle Lisgo

Rachel Margaret Lee

Paula Wright

Frank Styles

David Foggo

Ian Mac Connell

Christina Robertson

John Day

The Nine Henrys © Peter McAdam 2012

www.ninehenrys.com

for

Geordie Nettledyke

"He's Andre Breton mixed with Raymond Chandler, but a bit more illiterate"

                                                  Ex Teacher.

"He's a Geordie David Lynch and a paranoid to boot"

> A friend's flat I once bugged
> (they talked about other things
> which I won't go into here)

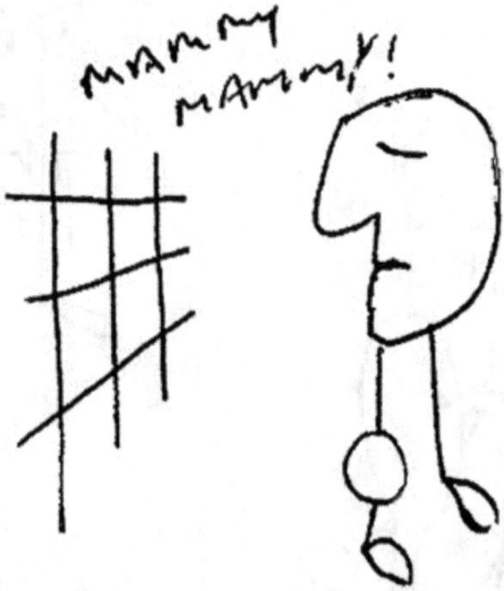
MAMMY
MAMMY!

After taking Anabolic Steriods for his under-developed right calf, Henry started hallucinating Al Jolson graphs

Henry would never wander from his daily chore of rubbing Blue Stilton on the skirting boards

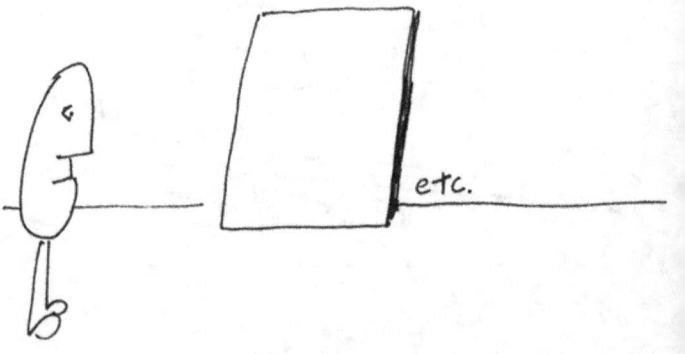

Henry was unimpressed with the Lazy Minimalist

Henry once remarked to a Hanging Finger
"Don't you give up comedy, young man".

Julian the King Prawn.

Reynolds transport Theorem
does my 'ead in

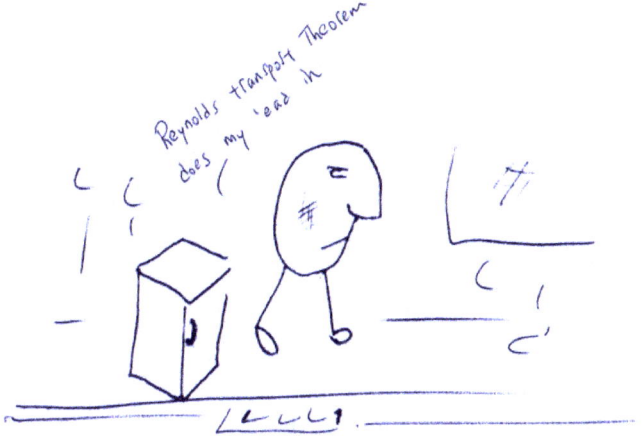

Having a 'fridge with a Doctorate in Fluid Dynamics was very embarrassing for Henry, especially in public places.

Henry was bizarrely afflicted with a staircase infection.

Henry had a peculiar allergy to Wordsworth.

Henry chanced upon a rock bun with a mobile 'phone,"Just go ahead with the deal you schmuck. I'll ring you back at ten".

The abstract poem.

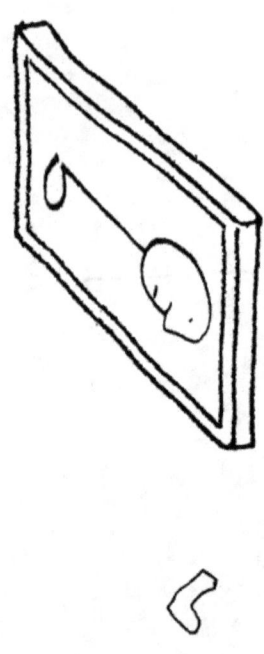

away from the sock

Henry's Kirk Douglas chin indentation transplant was too excessive.

Great!! Just what I always wanted! A Flying Snooker Cue.

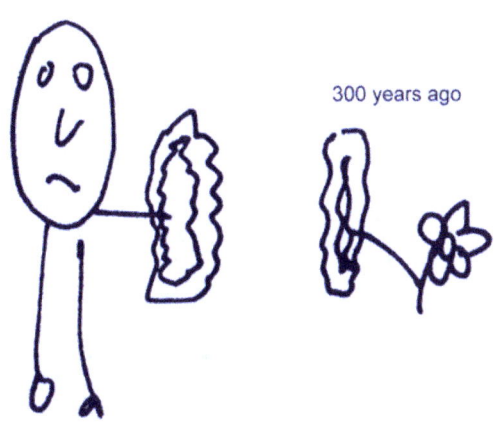

Time Travelling Daisy Picking

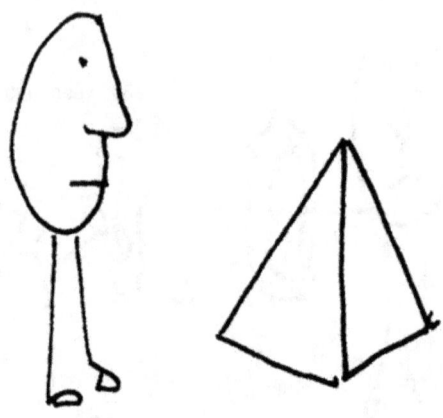

The Negative Dossier

Don't you want me baby?

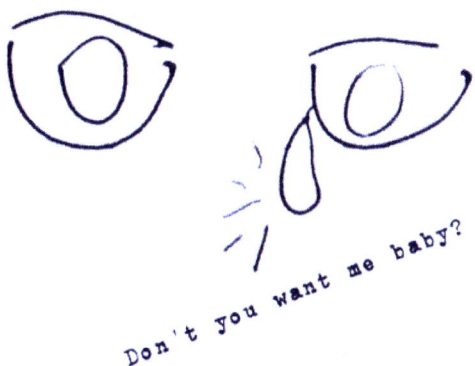

Karaoke Teardrop

These Mirrors are cool!!

Henry Burger

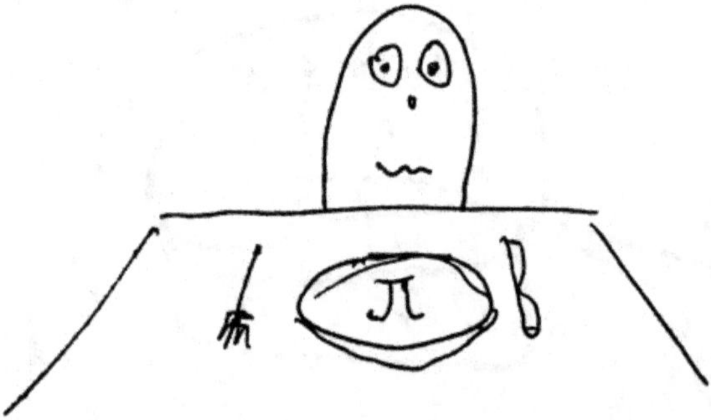
π

Pie for tea

Henry was once accosted by a beer-swilling humbucker pickup

A shy Henry on his First Date

Henry was proud of his leg garden

Conceptual Busking

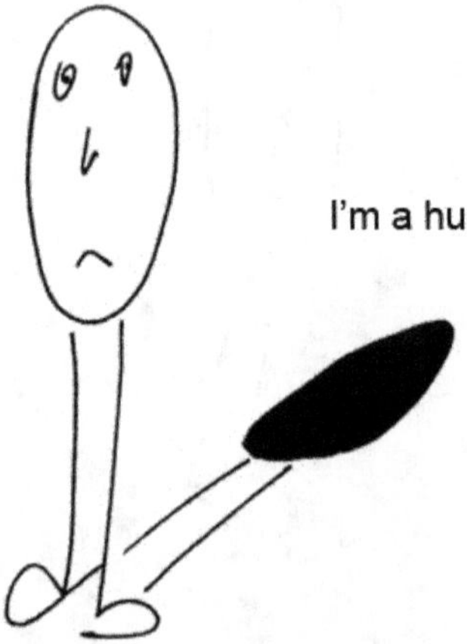

I’m a human of my former self

Bottom hat

Henry had a Clef Foot

Henry regretted turning out in his elephants

Henry's Christmas Dinner

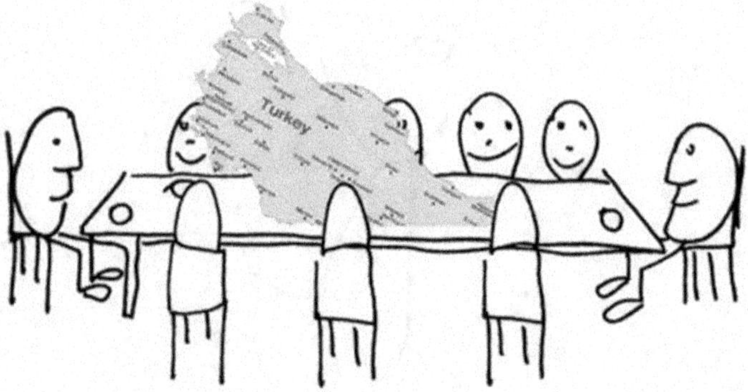
Turkey

"Istanbul looks tasty"

Henry tried his hand at Distance Learning

Henry was oblivious to the Great White Shark in his Guinness

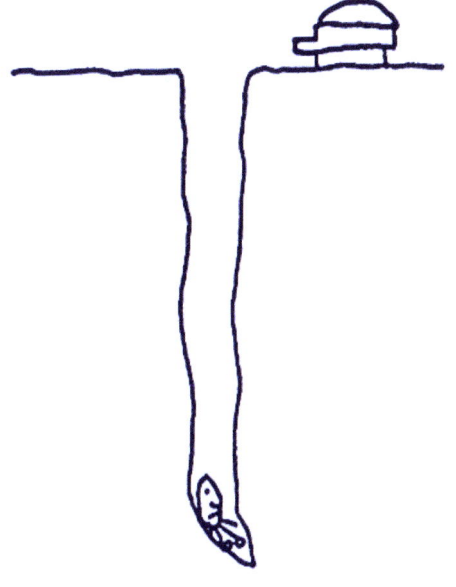

The Piano's Revenge

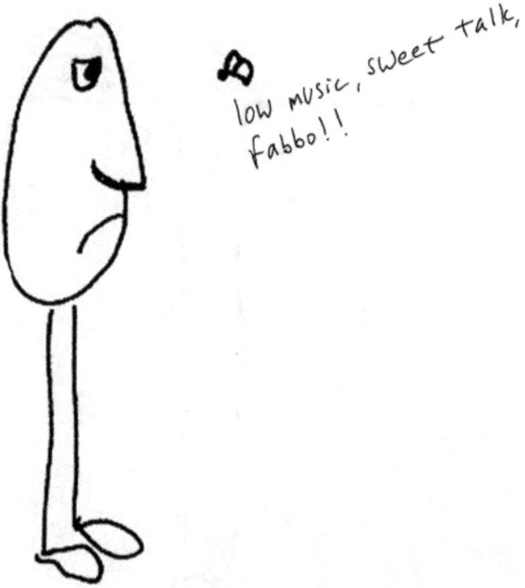
low music, sweet talk,
fabbo!!

Macbeth the domestic fly tutored Henry
In the art of getting girls

Francois the moody Existentialist Mirror
refused Henry his reflection

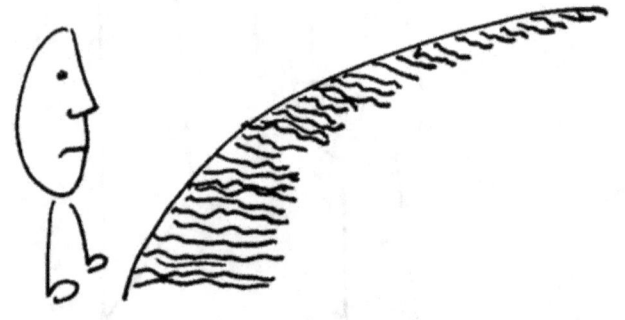

God's eyelash

The coincidence

Henry was perplexed by his first joint

Henry had an astounding beauty spot

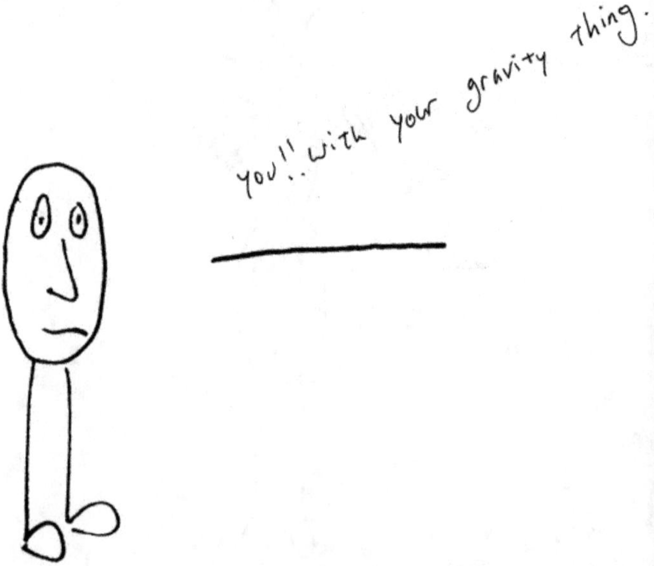
you!!..with your gravity thing.

The Horizontal Line insulted Henry on his verticalness

Henry had a bizarre fly problem

Henry's dreams were always above Sea Level

Henry would indulge in his favourite pastime
of levitating Yorkshire Puddings

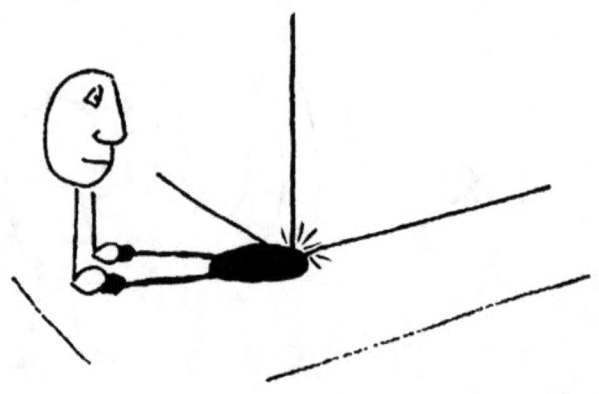

Henry's shadow bruised easily on corners

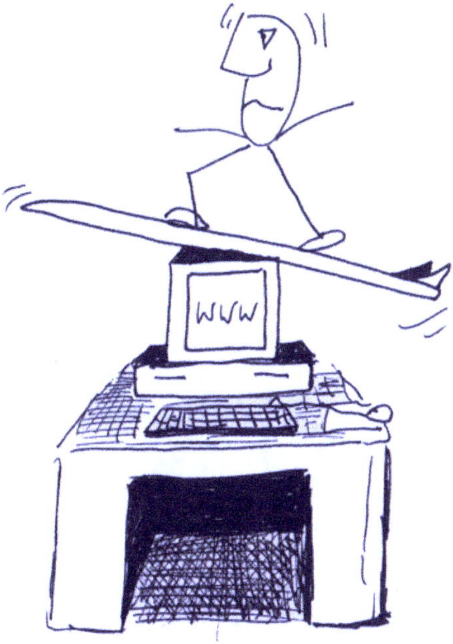
WWW

Henry surfs the web

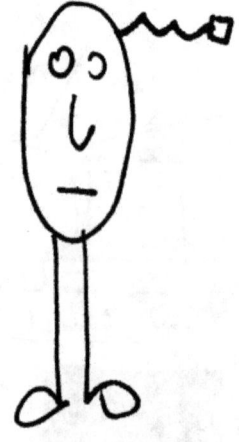

Corkscrew lobotomy

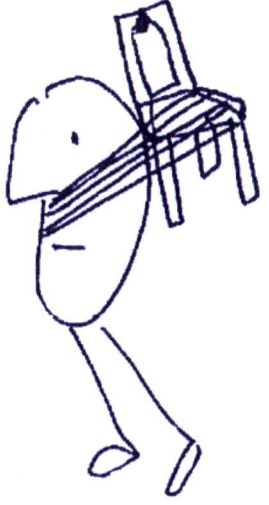

The Accidental Moustache Part One

The side effects of Nietzschian philosophy and Post-Hegelian dualism were taking their toll

'Fridge Tripping

The Schematics of Aspirin

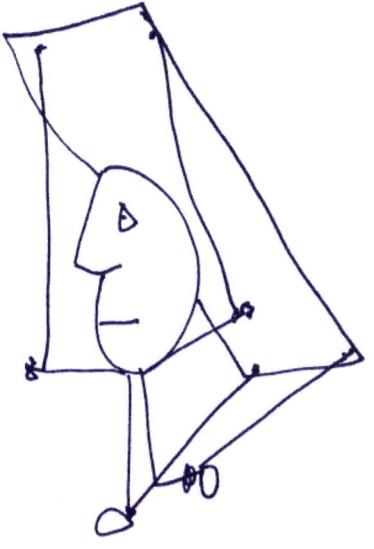

Sheet Metal Bondage

Henry told Henry, "Sort yourself out, you're a mess"

All these shoes I have to buy,
no one realises!

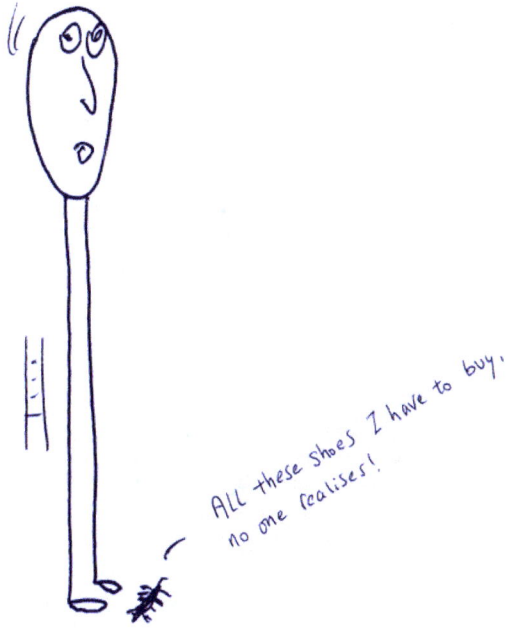

Henry would distance himself from a murmuring centipede

The Accidental Moustache Part Two

Haunted by Analogies

"But Everard, you'll never be a giraffe"

Henry took a part-time day job to pay for his studies
Sewing the shadows of clouds onto the side of buildings

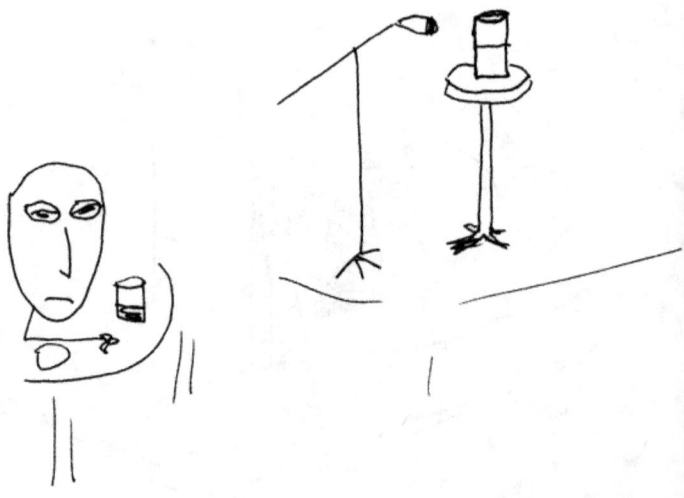

Alternative Comedy just wasn't Henry's scene

Henry's newly-acquired greyhound performed badly in the park

A Moon Cataract

...and the argument was settled

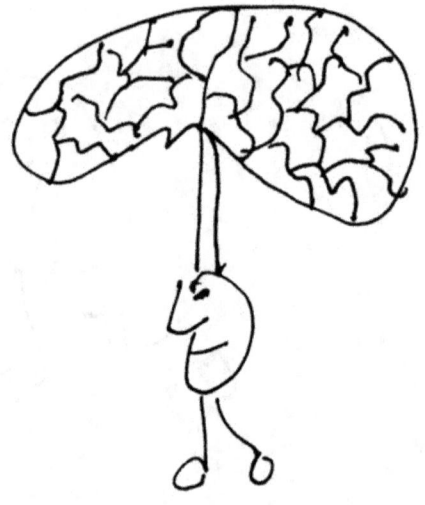

Henry has a brain extension

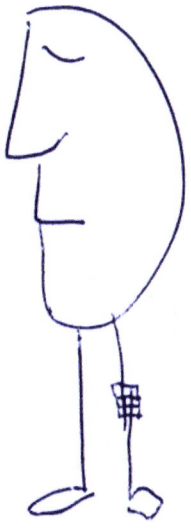

First Aid Waffle

Cold Sore Ascending

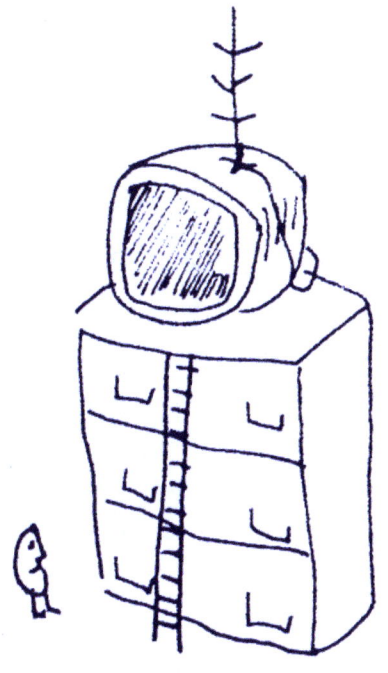

After losing his TV Remote, Henry's life
was beginning to be a bit of a chore

Henry's New Pool Table

Henry was living the high life

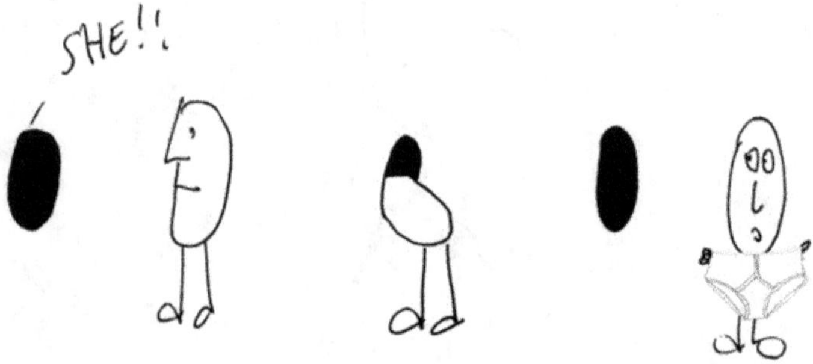
SHE!!

The Charles Aznavour Portal

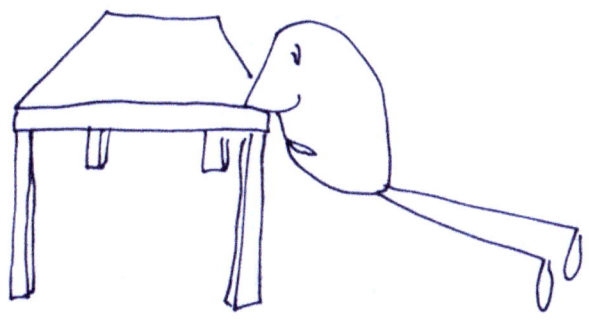

The Accidental Moustache Part Three

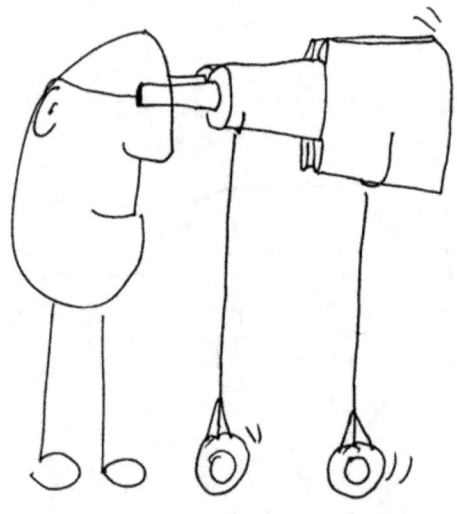

Henry marvelled at his new perambulative glasses
- Jupiter being his new neighbour

Henry once dated a false eyelash.
He knew her to be false because she lied about her job;
she wasn't the executive producer of a well-known sitcom!

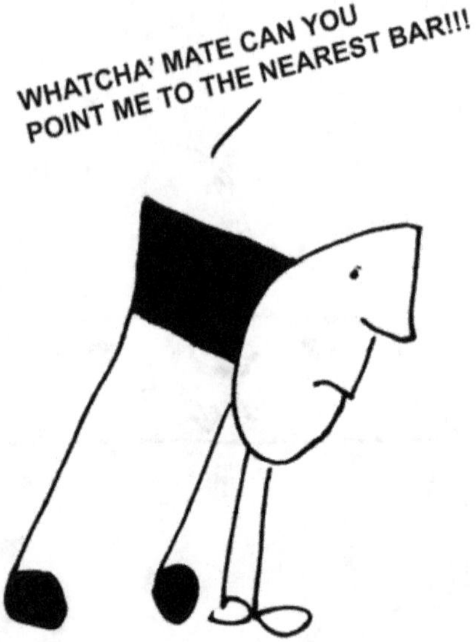
WHATCHA' MATE CAN YOU
POINT ME TO THE NEAREST BAR!!!

Henry was being leaned on by a clef

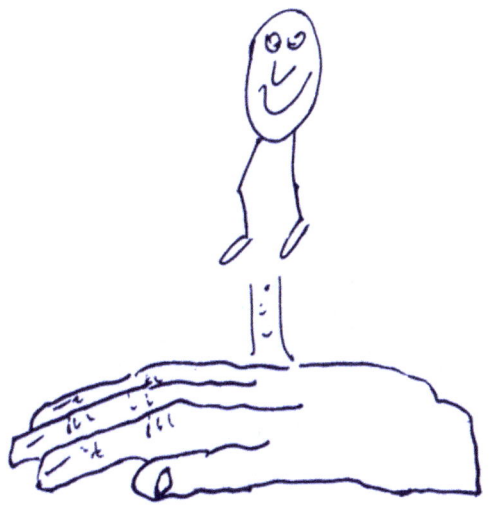

The Dead Hand Trampoline

Henry took the roof off, so when he's in, he's actually out!

"What do you think of my leg extensions?"
remarked Paulus the Butterfly

On Henry's birthday, few of his old mates turned up

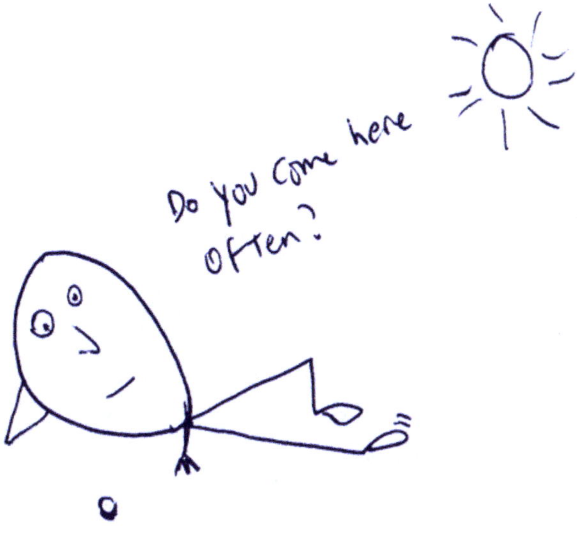
Do you come here often?

Henry leisurely seduces a lost coin

The wedge of Emmental spuriously denied the claims of it being an escapee

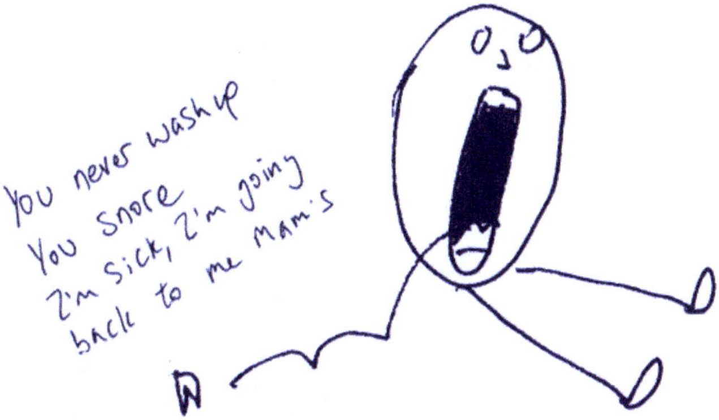
You never wash up
You snore
I'm sick, I'm going
back to me Mam's

Henry was relieved he was free of his nagging tooth

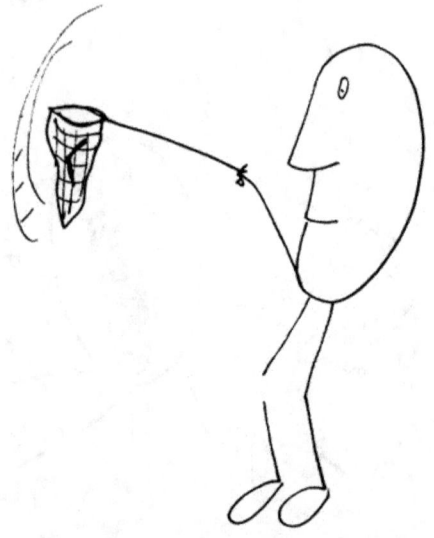

Henry caught his knee

WHASSUUPP!!!

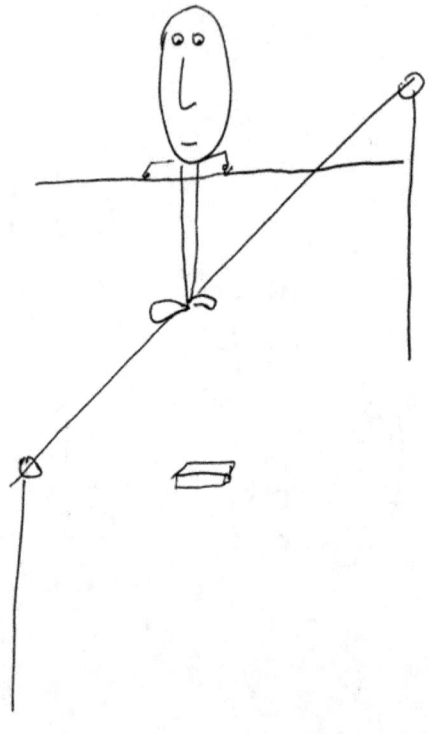

Henry fearlessly attempted to walk the tighrope over a ferocious shoebox

Henry was really getting into his book

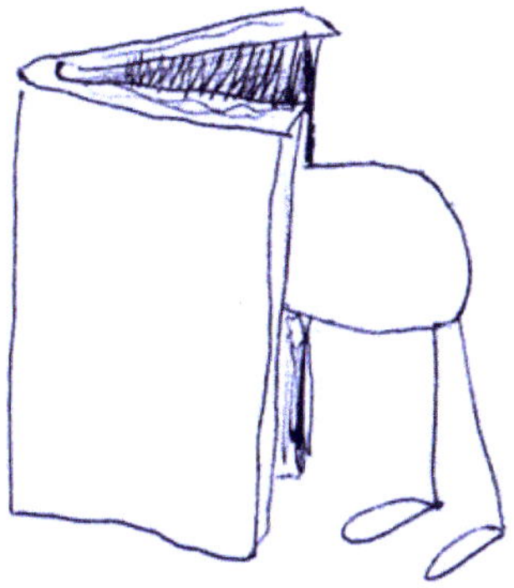

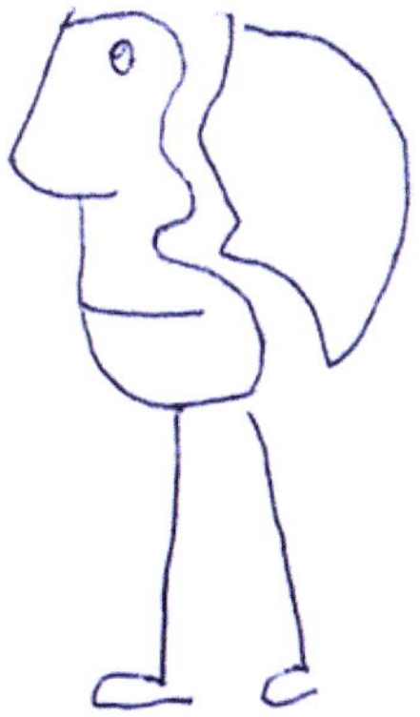

The fragmentation of Papua New Guinea

Beginning with his arms, Henry was turning into a Heritage Site

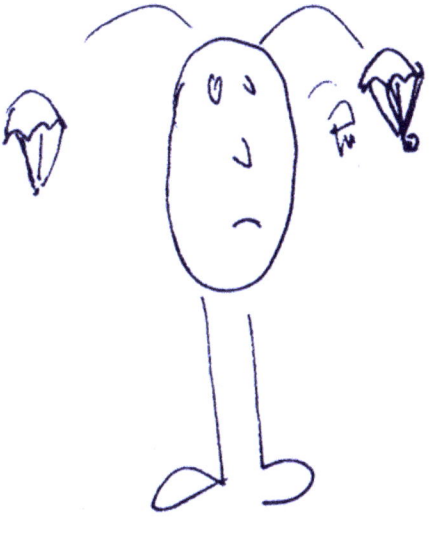

RAF Dickies

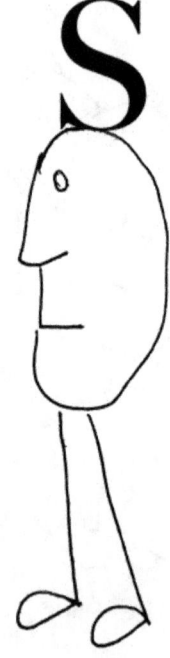

Henry consonantly wore a hat

Olga the Yoghurt Carton and Henry in Student Bar at Uni

OLGA: Do you think Muyerbridge exploited the narrative in Pre-Surrealist Cinema, or was he just mucking about with sequential planted cameras?

HENRY: Gee I guess, where's the toilets?

"'Hey, Marvin. What are you doing with that guy underneath your feet?"

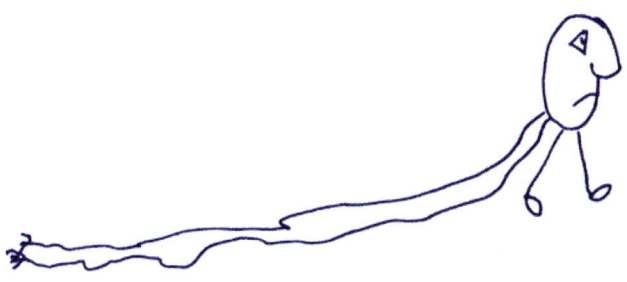

"Let go! Let Go" were the last words Henry heard
before he did his Bungee Jump

Retinal Judo

Haunted by Analogies

Making a Bacon Sandwich the Henry Way

Smooth evenly....   Oh!! Nice...

Watch you don't drip Pope Innocent X,
you'll never get it out of the carpet.

The Pineapple Cube Incident

The Accidental Moustache Part Four

Henry Island

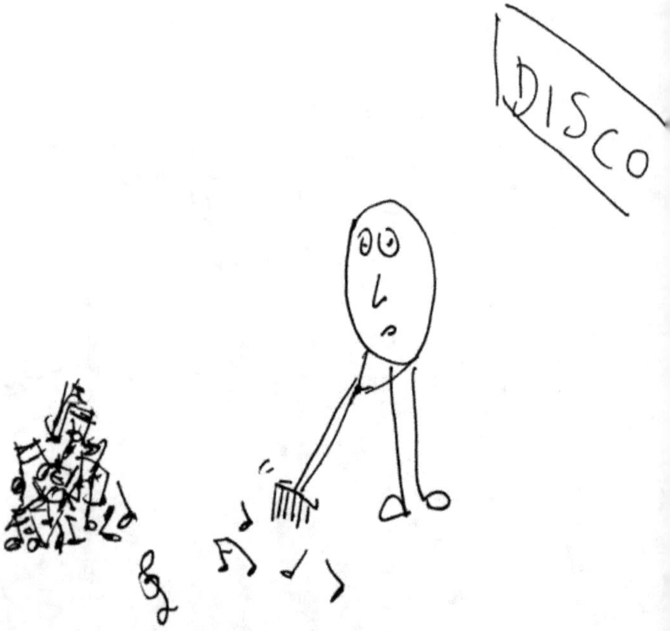
DISCO

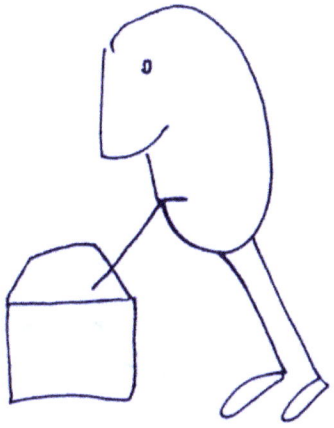

Raspberry Concrete Block

"Mmmm! Interesting...."

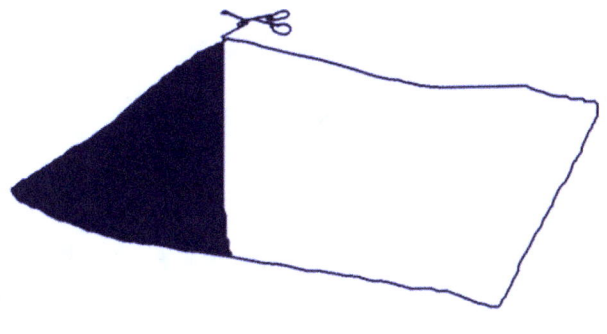

"Help!!"

Club foot

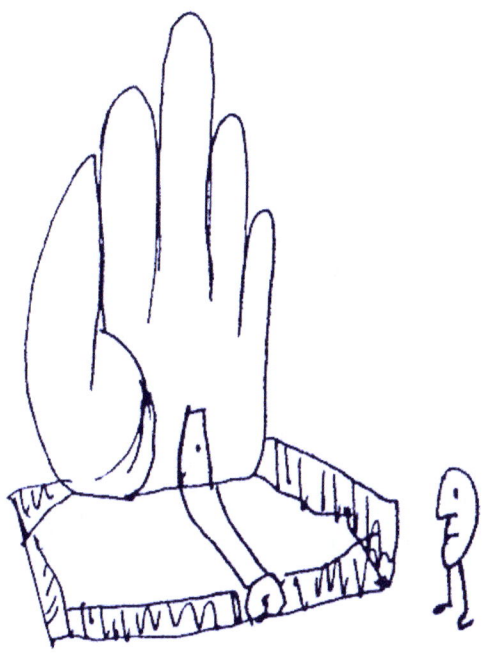

Henry's new home was in a handy area

"My name is Hermes Poppadopolis
and I am the Saviour Of The Universe"

Russian Henry

HENRY @ THE MOVIES

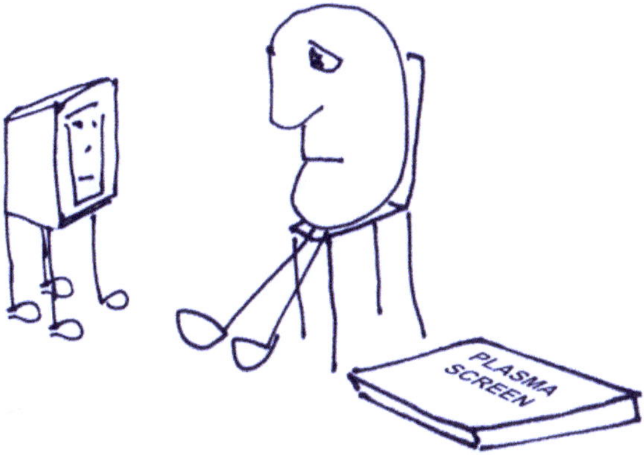

PLASMA
SCREEN

I'm not an Animal I am a Henry
and stop calling me "Dumbo"

""SURPRISE!!!...... I got you a RING"

"You talking to me?
I'm the only one here"

"Can you pipe down I'm trying to watch the TV"

With my droogs in the Korova trying to make up our rassoodocks, I viddied them drinking vollocet and synthmesc, ready for the old ultra-violence listening to Ludwig Van's 9th. All the malenky little hairs on plott endwise.
All very horrorshow.

""DO YOU SPEAK ENGLEEESH?"

1

"I've seen things you people wouldn't believe
Attack Ships on fire off the shoulder of Orion"

— Harrison.

2

"I watched C-beams glitter in the darkness at
Tannhauser Gate"

3

"All those moments... will be lost...in time like tears in the Rain... Time to die"

4

"... actually... I think I've got cramp"

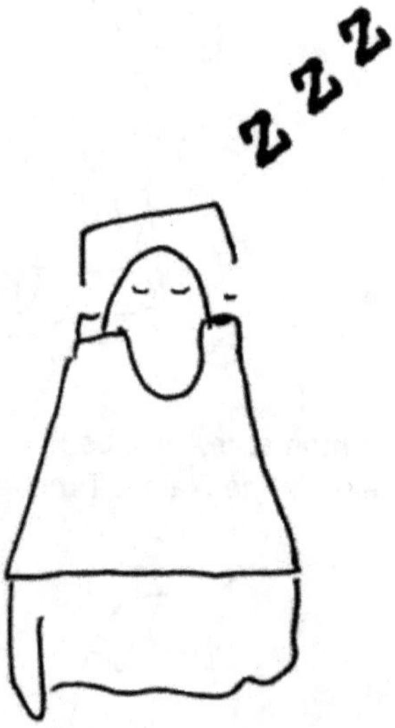
z z z

"Oh! My God! I had a nightmare
I was in a badly drawn cartoon"

1

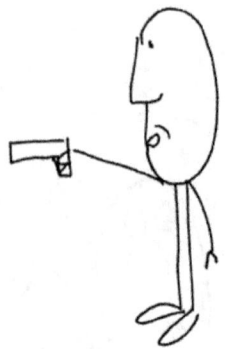

"I know what you're thinking punk.
You're thinking did he fire six shots
or only five?
Tell you the truth I've forgotten myself
in all this excitement"

2

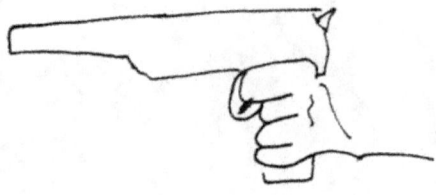

"This being a 44 Magnum the most powerful
hand gun in the world and would blow your
head clean off.
You should ask yourself a question.
Do I feel LUCKY?"

3

"Well do ya PUNK?"

4

"Erm!! I'll skip the Scratchcard and just pay for the crisps"

1

"Even the Jungle wanted him dead
thats who he took his orders from anyway"

2

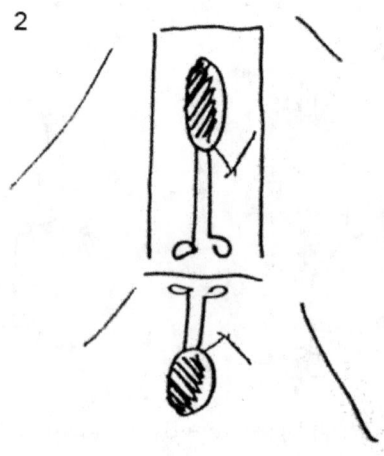

3

"Wheres my Pizza?"

4

'"Sorry no Pizza, but I got you a
Happy Henry Meal and a free balloon"

1

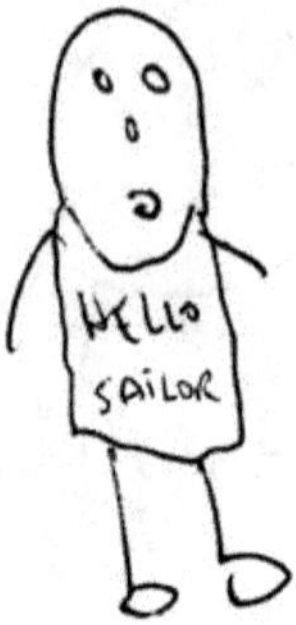
HELLO
SAILOR

"Colonel Jessop, did you order Code Red?"

2

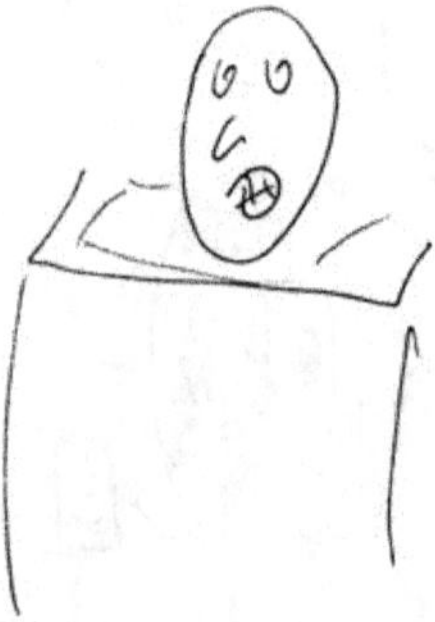

'"You want ANSWERS?"

3

"I think I am entitled... I want the TRUTH"

4

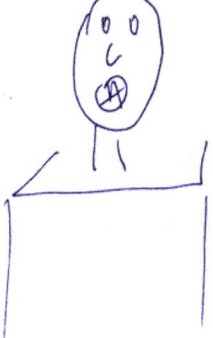

"'You can't handle RUTH, she's a canny lass and does a lot for Charity"

1

"OH MY GOD! Thats a bit elaborate"

2

'"But hey... it beats a Red Flag anyday. Surfs up"

3

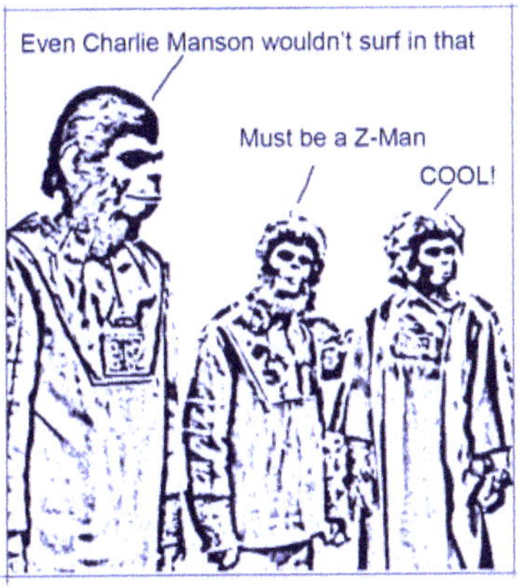
Even Charlie Manson wouldn't surf in that
Must be a Z-Man
COOL!

4

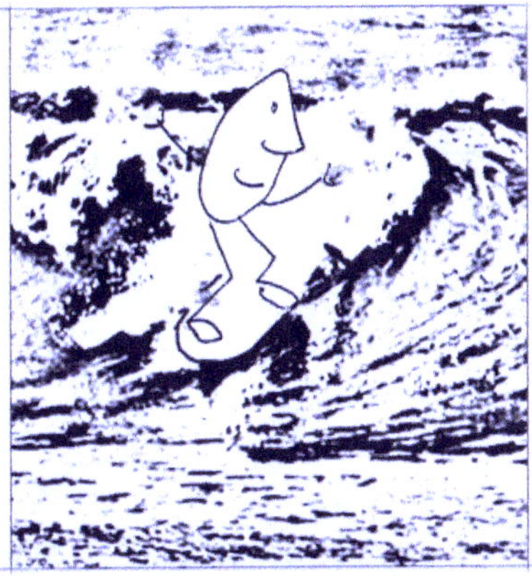

“”"It’s amazing what you can do
with a legless Ironing Board”

"WAITER! WAITER! There's a Film Noir in my Soup"

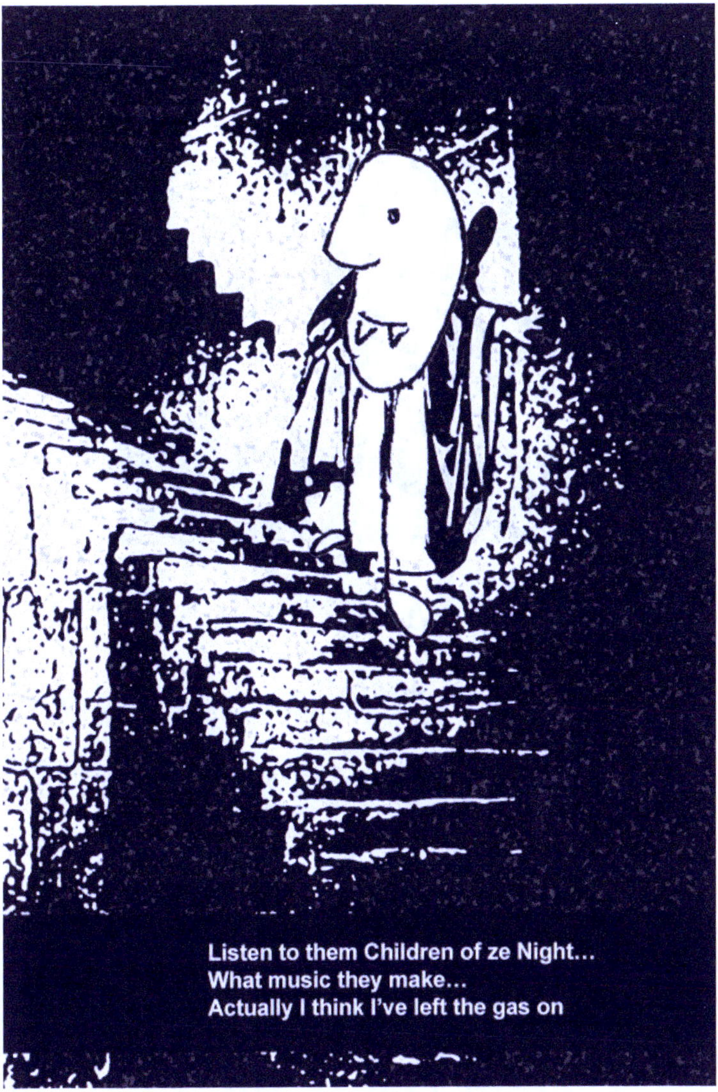
Listen to them Children of ze Night...
What music they make...
Actually I think I've left the gas on

authentic X·ray

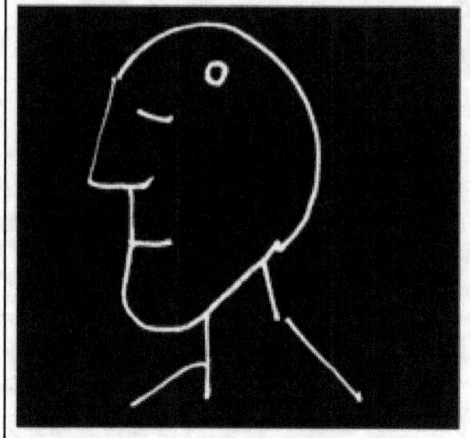

THE AUTHORS PEA NUT SIZED BRAIN FROM WHICH THE ADVENTURES OF THE NINE HENRYS EMERGE-

Peter McAdam was born in the early 60s, but reborn with the punk explosion of 1976. None of us really existed before then; that was his artistic birth:

The Big Cherrranggggg!

Of course, where he travelled to from there has as much to do with Marcel Duchamp as Malcolm McLaren! But at least initially, he was a hairy-jumpered, guitar-slinging, leather-jacketed punk rocker, from a council house in one of the toughest little mining villages outside of Durham; Washington, Tyne & Wear. I should know; I saw him then, at a *Murder the Disturbed* Saturday morning rehearsal in 1977, with his band. They looked like a cross between Sid Vicious, Wayne County & Jilted John. We fancied the same punk sirens and hung out at the village disco in Blue House Lane.

Then he disappeared till 1985, when I met him at a bus stop in Fatfield; we both looked more Beatnik by then. I had never really talked to him properly until that day at the bus stop, which would seal our great friendship for evermore. First thing I noticed about Peter was his childlike enthusiasm, and incredible knowledge; I mean, we were poorly educated sons of miners and factory girls, yet his hunger was his university.

His lack of competition, his grace, his ability to share and support; his periscope, highly unusual for a young man in such a harsh environment. I felt inspired in his presence (still do); I just have to think of Peter and his medicine pours through. We used to practice meeting up in lucid dreams, beyond the human-defined world: pulled it off a couple of times!

His spiritual/cosmic awareness, his powerful left brain, ability to think so far outside the box that he was back in it, outstanding mind: his first flirtations with Dada and Surrealism, both in poetry and art, would form a deep groove, the canyon of his life I would say, a beautiful canyon between Dali & Apollinaire.

His first art exhibition at Washington Arts Centre was where one of the works in particular stood out...'The Kiss', a mousetrap fully loaded and cocked on the wall, with some big ruby red kissable lips coloured in felt tips and cut out like a child as the bait, hilarious! And what a stir he created..... "This is not art!" etc. etc.

Peter McAdam was Banksy in 1985; his fave tool was the felt tip pen, but his conceptual grasp was at the highest level, a level you just can't teach: it has to come from another dimension, and his disability as far as copyist/photography-type drawing styles was purely an asset, still is and is perfectly in keeping with his Punk Rock ethos.

There are many people who can draw or play instruments who are not artists. Peter is a pure artist; whatever he dabbles with becomes art: language, film, nature...

I am honoured to celebrate with him 'The Nine Henrys', and call him my friend and brother...

In truth

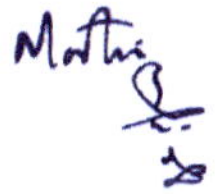

Martin Stephenson

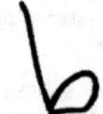

"Sorry... I'm a bit late"

www.ingramcontent.com/pod-product-compliance
Lightning Source LLC
LaVergne TN
LVHW051500070426
835507LV00022B/2851